THE SUCCESS FACTOR

by
FRED GOOD

University Publishers
P. O. Box 3571
Chattanooga, Tennessee 37404

Library of Congress Card Catalog Number 85-50414
ISBN 0-931117-02-X

DEDICATION

To the most important people in my life—My wife Eloise and our four children, Steve, Becky, Roger and Patti.

PREFACE

Ask any young person if he plans to succeed in life, and he will say "yes." However, only five out of a hundred will be self-supporting at retirement age. The rest will be dependent on family or social security. Living in a land of opportunity, they will somehow fail to comprehend the elements that will guide them to success.

Most of these will begin their career with great expectations, but as marriage and children come along, they will settle down to "job security." The more ambitious will spend a lifetime searching for an elusive formula that will guarantee success. They will attend motivational seminars, read success books, and attend courses designed to enhance their memory and personality. They will learn that a positive attitude, enthusiasm, imagination, and goals play an important part in life's game.

But is there a success factor? A formula so

perfect that it can not fail? Yes, there is such a key. A secret? Not really. It has remained a secret only because we have failed to grasp that which should have been apparent.

This is the story of one man who grasped the secret.

THE SUCCESS FACTOR

It was in a small community park that I first saw him—a tall man in a disheveled pin stripe suit, with salt and pepper hair, an unshaved face and angry eyes. I was sitting on a bench across the walkway from the creek that wended through the park. It was about eleven-thirty. The sun was shining. A slight breeze ruffled the leaves. Not far away, two lovers were spreading a picnic under an ancient oak. On the bench to my right, two squirrels ran playfully back and forth across the top board. To the left, some kids were kicking a blue-green plastic ball, the type you get in a supermarket. The song of a mockingbird penetrated the air. The whisper of water and the laughter of children brought tranquility to the park.

I first heard his cane tapping the concrete walkway as he came toward me. He weaved slightly and used the cane to support his steps.

As he neared the squirrels, his cane swept out across the top of the bench. The creatures scrambled for safety as the man chuckled softly. One of the children darted in front of the man, chasing the ball. I heard him curse the child as he walked on.

I made my way out of the park to Ruby's Cafe, near the entrance. He was sitting two tables down from me. I had already been served before a waitress even approached him for his order.

"How do you get waited on around here," he growled.

The waitress ignored his comment. "What will you have?" she asked.

During the following few months I saw him several times. I never once saw him make a friendly gesture. I never saw him walking with or conversing with anyone. His clothing was not old; it was slept in. It was not ragged, just dirty. His hair was apparently immune to a comb. But while he had little time for others and little money for personal needs, he apparently had funds for liquor. During that summer I saw him several times in the park or, occasionally, on the sidewalk, passed out next to his wine bottle. He was a human derelict.

It seemed difficult to imagine this man as a baby sleeping in the arms of his mother or as a boy playing catch in the yard with his dad. Neither could I perceive of him as a first grader, anxious to please his teacher. I could not help but wonder what had gone wrong. Had his home provided the garden for sprouting and growing an angry old man? Had his parents never complimented him or encouraged him? Had his business or marriage failed? I never had the courage to ask. He would probably have only cursed me.

As the leaves fell, I realized I never saw him anymore. I wondered if he had passed out in some squalid apartment house, never to revive again.

The following April, on one of those days when it is impossible to sit still in an office, I left early for lunch. Ambling through the park, I stood for a moment by the brook, watching the ducks swim by. I turned to observe someone strolling toward me. The man was walking erect. I could hardly believe it. It was the same man I had observed staggering through the park the previous summer. There was no cane. He was dressed handsomely and groomed neatly. He was smiling.

As the gentleman approached a gathering of pigeons, he reached into his pocket, pulled out a sack, and spread a handful of seeds in a clear spot on the ground. As he passed me, he threw a friendly wave. On beyond me a blond-headed little boy was crying and looking in the grass.

"What's the trouble, son?" the man asked.

"I lost my quarter," the boy sobbed.

The man pointed in my direction. "Have you looked there behind you?" While the boy turned, the man took a coin from his pocket and tossed it in the grass.

"There it is." He pointed again.

The lad picked up the coin. "Thank you, Sir," the boy smiled. The man continued on his way, and the boy skipped down the sidewalk, still smiling.

I was awed. The man was a new creature. I walked behind him through the park and into Ruby's Cafe.

"Good morning, Ruby," he greeted the lady behind the register.

"Good morning, Bill. Your party is waiting for you," she replied as she walked with him to a table occupied by twelve well-dressed men.

As they walked, the man placed his hand on Ruby's shoulder. "Young lady, I certainly appreciate your lovely smile this morning."

Her smile became broader. "Gentleman," she said as they reached the table. "This is the man you've been waiting for." They stood and applauded as he took the vacant seat at the head of the table.

I couldn't make out any of their conversation. I tried, though, because frankly, I could not understand the mystery. I could see that "Bill" did most of the talking. Everyone seemed to listen intently.

Bill received far better service than anyone else

in the restaurant. Every waitress in the cafe made some attempt to please him. One would refill his water glass, another the coffee cup. To each he would make some remark about their hairdo or dress or smile.

Actually, I did not enjoy my meal that day, not that there was anything wrong with the food or the service; I was just absorbed in the mystery. Even though others asked for his autograph, I did not want to interrupt his meeting, but I was determined to make an appointment to talk with him. I was compelled to find out who Bill was and, more importantly, how his life had been transformed.

Ruby walked to his table and spoke to him. "Bill, your limousine is waiting." He stood and apologized to his guests. They all stood and walked with him to the register. The crowd frustrated my attempts to get near him. Finally, we were out on the street, and I had pushed my way to his side.

Cautiously, I reached out to touch his arm. He turned and gave me a warm handshake. With transparent blue eyes, he looked directly at me and asked what he could do for me. I introduced myself and told him that, although I didn't even know him, I needed to talk with him. He told me that his name was William Henry Sebastian, and that he would be happy to talk to me, but he had to catch a plane for Europe. At this point the chauffer came around and opened the door.

"We are running late, sir."

Sebastian took the driver's hand and asked how he was doing. "How is the wife, Mary, and those great little kids of yours?" he continued.

"Fine sir, just fine," the driver responded as Sebastian got into the car.

In desperation I reopened the door. "Sir, please allow me to ride to the airport so that I can ask you a few questions and ease my inquisitive mind."

"Sure, hop in," he agreed.

The airport was only a few blocks from the cafe, so I knew I would have to talk fast. As soon as the limousine was moving, I began. "Mr. Sebastian, I certainly don't intend to embarrass you, but I am convinced that I remember you from several months ago. After seeing you today and observing your behavior and attitude toward people, I believe I am looking at an entirely different man, yet with the same body."

Sebastian willingly responded, "What you say is true. I can tell you frankly that I am a man re-born. I was a drunken, miserable, degenerate only a few months ago. I owe the change to the fact that my life was transformed in a matter of minutes. I would like to tell you how the change came about. What I will reveal will astound you, for you see, I have been given the secret of secrets—the master key that unlocks the door to life's greatest rewards, success and happiness."

I listened, certain that William Henry Sebastian could reveal a mystery of great importance. I felt "chosen" you might say, to be there at that moment to hear him speak. I could hardly wait to hear his story.

At that moment the car pulled up at the airport terminal. Sebastian stepped from the car. "I apologize, sir, but I must leave at once. I will be in Europe for awhile, and I am not certain when I will be back. However, if you are interested in hearing my story, give me your card. I promise to contact you when I return."

I gave him my card and watched as he walked into the terminal. I was almost limp with disappointment. Would I ever see William Henry Sebastian again?

I don't believe a day passed during the next three months that I did not think of Sebastian and wonder about his transformation. Whenever I would see a drunk or derelict, my thoughts would be of him. If I came near the park or walked into Ruby's Cafe, Sebastian flashed through my mind.

Finally, in late June, a lady called from Chicago. She was calling for William Henry Sebastian. "Could you have lunch with Mr. Sebastian tomorrow at Ruby's Cafe?" she asked.

I agreed readily, "It would be my pleasure!"

"Mr. Sebastian will meet you at 12:00 noon," she said.

The following day I walked into the cafe about fifteen minutes early. I noticed a beggar panhandling in front of the cafe. The beggar approached Sebastian with his hand extended. Instead of placing a coin in his palm, Sebastian took his hand and gave it a gentleman's shake. He placed his other hand on the man's shoulder and guided him toward the front door of the cafe. As they entered, Sebastian asked the beggar to be seated on one of the stools at the counter. Sebastian then spoke to the waitress, requesting that the man be permitted to order a meal of his choice. Sebastian would pick up the tab.

Then Sebastian came to my table and shook my hand. "I've looked forward to seeing you again and telling you my story. You seemed so eager to hear it." He asked if I would have the time to finish lunch before he began the story, that we walk to a quiet place in the park so we would not again be disturbed. I agreed. As we ate, Sebastian talked about his time in Europe. He had also gone to the spot on the earth that he most wanted to see—the Holy Land.

After lunch we walked to the bench near the center of the park where I had first seen him. Sebastian began to reveal his story.

"I was born into a prosperous family. I was the

only child. My father and mother had both come from a poor childhood. My father would boast, from time to time, about being a self-made man. He started a small grocery store at the age of twenty, five years before he married. By the time wedding bells rang for him and Mother, he had expanded the business into a giant supermarket. I was born two years later.

"From my earliest memory, I can recall my father boasting to friends that his son would never have to work like he did. He felt he had been 'looked down on' during his childhood and he was determined that nobody would look down on me. He made sure that no kid on the street had better toys than William Henry. Looking back, I can see that I was a spoiled, arrogant child. I did not quite understand why I had so few friends. I remember asking, 'Mommy, why don't the other kids like me?'

" 'They are just jealous of you, darling,' she would reply.

"I didn't do well in school simply because I didn't try. When the report card came with the bad grades or the teacher sent a note home about my behavior, I always seemed to be able to convince my parents that for some reason or other the teacher just didn't like me—that she was out to get me. Instead of recognizing that my story was merely an excuse for failure, my parents set out to get even with the teacher. They would call the principal, seeking to have the teacher fired. When that did not work, they would shift me from one school to another. Time after time, I continued to fail, blaming it on the teacher, or the kids in my class, or the lack of opportunity to do what I wanted to do. Each time my parents, no doubt believing that they were doing what was best, permitted me to ignore the reality that I was the source of my own problems.

"My father's business continued to prosper. His single supermarket soon grew into a chain of luxury supermarkets. While my father spent little time at home, he always made sure that I had plenty of money. As soon as I was old enough for a driver's license, my Dad bought me the fanciest T-bird in town. I believed that money could buy anything. My date book was filled. As I roared about town, I became the envy of the guys. I was the cock of the walk. When I would throw a party, the neighborhood would turn out because we would hire a band, hand out flowers and gifts to the girls, and serve caviar and champagne. Once in a while, I would talk for a minute or two about my delight that all my friends had come to the party which would always bring on whistling and applause.

"I finished high school and enrolled in Rutgers. However, college interfered with living, and I soon dropped out. Why did I need college anyway? My father hadn't even finished grade school. He had made it. At the time it seemed silly for me to spend my time learning a profession or planning for the future. After all, my father was able to supply all the money that I would ever need. I did not feel the slightest desire to become responsible. During my early twenties I lived the life of a jet-setter who had nothing more to do than spend every waking hour partying, boozing and trying to seduce every woman who ventured into our circle of friends.

"My parents would caution me about my wild living, but they contributed to and condoned my life-style by supplying an unending conduit of money. By the age of twenty-four I had been around the world and gorged on every luxury available to man. I had contributed nothing to society or to my own upkeep.

"Up to this time I had never had a lasting relationship with a woman. I thought the opposite sex was a vessel to be used and then discarded. But a dramatic thing happened at this period of my life that left a scar and an emptiness that I had not known before.

"I was invited to a wedding in Nashville, Tennessee. This was in 1955. After the wedding, with a few drinks under my belt, I decided to rent a car and see the mountains.

"It was late in the evening when I began to drive, with the aid of a fifth of scotch. I lost my sense of direction as I drove further into the hills. It was January, and patches of snow and ice were visible in the mountains. As darkness began to fall, I turned off on a dirt road that was wet and slick. It began to rain and sleet; the car was slipping and sliding all over the road. And to add to the difficulty, the ground began to freeze.

"I reached the top of a steep hill and began to descend a very steep grade. The car began to slide completely out of control. I realized that I was in trouble, but the liquor had dulled my mind to the immediate and grave danger that lay ahead. The vehicle must have reached a speed of sixty miles an hour as it weaved and slid to the bottom of the hill. I gunned the engine, attempting to straighten it in the road. The car reached the bottom of the hill, slid into a ditch on the left-hand side and stopped with a jolt as the front slammed into a wall of red clay.

"That was the last thing I remembered, but as I learned later, my head had hit the steel roof support and this blow sent me into a coma that was to last more than two days. The next thing I recalled was opening my eyes in a small room illuminated by a kerosene lamp. My head was bursting with pain. I could see the image of three people around the bed. 'Where am I?' I asked.

"A soft female voice answered that I was in the home of Daniel and Sara Webster. 'I am their daughter, Leilani.'

"My vision was blurred, but I can recall to this day the warmth and caring attitude that prevailed in that room.

"I asked how I had arrived in their home. Leilani explained that some of the men had spotted my car early on the morning of the accident. Finding me in an unconscious state, they had carried me to the nearest home. These people had cared enough for a total stranger to bring me into their home and take turns sitting by my bed, waiting for me to awaken.

"They had tried to reach a doctor, but since there was no telephone in that area of Tennessee and the roads were too rough to travel, they could only sit and wait.

"I felt the top of my head to find that a large spot had been shaved. Leilani told me that this had to be done to close a two-inch gash. She had sewn it up with a sewing needle and thread.

"As my vision began to clear, I could see the faces of these strangers who had taken me in. Daniel Webster was a tall thin man in his fifties. He was balding, and his face was narrow and furrowed. His skin was weathered. He wore blue bib overalls and worn brogan shoes, faded and cracked. I could smell the tobacco as he puffed away on a cracked old pipe.

"Sara was a small woman. I figured her age at about forty-five, but hard work and weather had made deep furrows in her brow. Her hair was dark with a few iron-gray strands. It was pulled back from her face and twisted into a ball on the back of her head. She wore a calico dress reaching all the way to the floor and buttoned at the neck.

"I felt my addled mind might be playing tricks on me, but Leilani's face seemed to be the most beautiful face I had ever seen. I cannot describe the depth and sparkle of her emerald green eyes. Her hair was dark and long, reaching to her waist, straight with the hair slightly curled at the ends.

"Her name was like music, and it fit this lovely mountain girl. I learned later that the unusual Hawaiian name came from a song that Sara had heard before Leilani was born.

"The full blue print dress she was wearing could not hide the beautiful body. Every movement revealed a supple beauty and grace. She was about eighteen years of age.

"I tried to get up, but the pain in my chest was

so great I just moaned. Leilani said that I probably had broken ribs. I was not able to get out of bed for several days, and Leilani was near me most of this time. She prepared the meals, washed my face and cared for me as I had never been cared for before.

"After several days I was up walking around. Mr. Webster had taken his mules and pulled my car from the ditch to the yard. I was surprised at the slight damage that had been done.

"The car was drivable, and I told the Websters that I had accepted too much of their hospitality and should drive back to the city. They would not hear of this and demanded that I stay until fully recovered. I was thrilled. I was falling in love. I was completely captivated by Leilani. She was also falling in love with me. One evening we walked up the mountain to a cliff. We sat on a huge rock and looked far below to a whirling pool of water at the bottom of a high waterfall. The beauty and peace of that place was indescribable. I first kissed Leilani at this spot. Each day we would return. I fell deeply in love. Leilani was with me constantly. She said she couldn't live without me.

"I stayed at the Websters' long after I had healed. For more than a month I lived in that enchanted valley. I met all the relatives and most of the neighbors. Each Saturday night the neighbors would gather with fiddles, guitars and banjos for hours of sometimes soulful and sometimes spiritual mountain music.

"On Sundays we went to church. It was a new experience for me, and a little disconcerting, but the people were simple and sincere. I was willing to tolerate these services just to be near Leilani. The people talked about Jesus and the Bible as if it were really important, an idea alien to my whole life. I respected these people and their faith in spite of myself.

"Some of the people made stronger impressions on me than others. One of my favorite mountaineers was a brother of Daniel Webster. His name was Isaac. He was tall and skinny, with a large Adam's apple and no teeth. He reminded me of Andy Gump in the funny paper. Old Isaac was a real comic. He could tell a simple little joke with such emotion and facial distortion that everyone was laughing way before the punch line. I felt accepted by those people.

"Leilani and I were inseparable. On my last day in the mountains, we walked up to the cliff that overlooked the waterfall and river far below. As I sat with my arm around this simple girl, I felt that I could never be happy without her. I asked her to marry me. As we walked down the mountain, I told Leilani that I would drive back to Nashville and fly on to Chicago to make preparations for bringing her back with me. I told her to get all her things together because I would be back within a month to marry her and to take her to Chicago.

"I can still see her tear-filled eyes as she stood beside her parents waving goodbye."

Sebastian paused. The music of children playing in the park was a counter note to his sorrow. He continued.

"You cannot imagine how many nights I have lain awake thinking of that final tearful goodbye and of what I would give to have had another chance to caress my only love, to kiss those innocent lips again.

"But it was not to be. I was in Chicago the next evening, and my intentions were to drive home and break the news of my marriage to my parents. Driving from the airport, I stopped at the country club for dinner and a drink. My misfortune was to run into a group of my jet set friends. I was introduced to a beautiful young blonde.

"The image of beautiful Leilani began to blur with all the booze and fancy living. Before I even told my parents, I decided that Leilani, 'backwoods girl', would not fit into the sophisticated city life. I rationalized that it would not work for either Leilani or myself. I imagined my parents thinking that I would be out of my mind to marry a simple mountain girl. I could not bear to think of the laughter and ridicule of my friends.

"For the next year I really lived it up, or so I thought. I flew all over Europe with my friends. There was not, however, an evening that I did not think of Leilani. I would often drown my misery in another drink or another woman.

"A year passed and I could restrict my conscience no longer. I had to see Leilani. I told my parents about my romance in the mountains and how I had promised to return to Leilani

within a month, how I had tried to forget her for more than a year, only to have her deep green eyes haunt every dream. They thought I had lost my mind, but I flew out of Chicago that night and arrived in Nashville. I rented a car the next morning and drove toward Leilani's home.

"It was early evening as I drove down the narrow dirt road toward the Websters' home. I saw old Isaac Webster walking along the road up ahead. I stopped and smiled as he walked up to the car. The old man was not smiling. I asked him about himself and about Leilani. His mouth began to quiver and he began to cry. 'You don't know, Mr. 'Bastion?'

" 'Don't know what?' I asked.

" 'Why, Mr. 'Bastion, after you lef', Leilani would walk up and down this road thinkin' she would meet you comin' back fer her. After a month or more she lost all hope, she did. She got so she wouldn't eat, jus' grievin' herself to death. I never seen nothin' like it. You stole her heart, you did.

" 'She would walk to the cliff most every day

and sit and stare. 'Bout six months ago she walked to the cliff and didn't come back. Dan and Sara were afraid to go up and look. I walked up, and I jus' knew what I was gonna see when I looked over that cliff. Sir, the broken body of that sweet Christian girl was layin' on that big rock at the bottom of the fall. It was awful, Mr. 'Bastion. Everyone in the valley is still mournin'.

" 'It's bes', Mr. 'Bastion, that you don't go down there. You'll only make things worse for poor Dan and Sara.'

"At this time the old man broke down and cried like a baby. As he walked away, he was shaking his head and saying, 'Go back, go back.'

"I was in a state of shock. What had I done? 'Sweet Leilani—God, let this be a nightmare,' I thought. I must have sat in the middle of the road for fifteen minutes before I finally turned the car around and drove recklessly back to Nashville.

"I had destroyed the only person in the world who had shown me real love. I wept for most of the next three days. I had blamed myself at the beginning, but in order to ease my torment, I began to turn my anger toward God. I began to blame him.

"This tragedy should have caused me to examine my selfish life. It, however, had the opposite effect. It hardened me.

"The year that I reached my twenty-sixth birthday, my father died unexpectedly of a heart attack. Mother lived only four months after his death. The entire family estate went to me. I spent little time mourning their passing. My first reaction was the recognition that with the inheritance of Dad's business I would undoubtedly be the wealthiest person in town. I was anxious to get my hands on Dad's money. I sold the entire supermarket chain.

"Overcome by the money at my disposal, a slight air of responsibility entered my life. I looked around for a way to invest a part of my fortune. I finally decided to try the stock market. With a knowledgeable broker guiding me, I soon began to reap a harvest of profits. Commodities became my specialty. Thanks to my broker, John Anderson, I became known as the man who never missed. People were seeking my advice on investments. John Anderson and I formed a brokerage consulting partnership. At the peak of our partnership we employed more than thirty brokers.

"We were succeeding beyond our greatest expectations. People from all across the nation and from every profession were gladly paying for our advice. Although John Anderson was the real brain, I began to believe that it was me who had providence on my side. Because of the rapid rise of the business, I imagined that through some strong mystic power, my personal investments and advice were close to infallible. I owned a plane and a yacht. I married a beautiful, sophisticated, socially-prominent woman. We threw the biggest and grandest parties. The yacht had a full-time captain and crew. To the delight of our customers and friends, we set sail at least once a month for a weekend of partying as we cruised to one of the off-shore islands or far out to sea to fish and sunbathe.

"While I had everything that money could buy, I was miserable. I was constantly searching for things that would bring happiness, but the more things I bought, the more places I went, and the more things I did, the less satisfaction I received. The things I thought would make me happy always turned to ashes in my mouth. I never gave much thought to the basic rules that govern success. In a way, the challenge had been removed from my life since everything had always been provided for me.

"My partner, John Anderson, was an opposite sort of fellow from me. He was reserved, certainly not the party type. As I said before, Anderson was the brains behind our operation. Nonetheless, my ego and aggressive personality enabled me to become the dominant figure in our firm. I constantly projected myself out front while Anderson was content to remain in the background. As a result, I often reaped the credit for Anderson's decision making. Oblivious to Anderson's contribution, many of our clients thought that I was a business genius.

"Anderson was successful because he studied markets and always invested his funds and that of our clients with the recognition that the value of an investment might fall even though it was most likely to rise. His investments were carefully chosen and diversified. Anderson utilized a formula that he developed which revealed when to buy and when to sell. Regardless of rumor or the market forcasts of others, Anderson would never vary from his formula. It worked.

"As our business prospered and I received most of the credit, I felt less need to rely solely upon Anderson's conservative strategy. Rejecting his advice, I began to gamble large sums of both my own funds and that of our clients on highly speculative ventures. Despite the fact that several of these risky investments did not turn out too badly, Anderson told me that we would have to have a parting of ways if I continued to increase the share of our investment funds allocated into speculative areas. I jumped at the chance to part with Anderson. Scoffing at his scholarly approach, I went my separate way. Most of our former clients went with me, substantially reducing the investment funds under the direction of Anderson. I began to listen to the rumor mill and the 'inside information' guys instead of sticking to an intelligent program. I was fortunate for a while, but as quickly as I had piled it up, my empire and the fortunes of many of those whom I advised began to crumble. I tried to counter the losses by risking larger amounts of capital. As the Dow

Jones averages plummeted during the last half of 1974, I didn't have the brains to get out. I was losing my self-confidence. I began to drink heavily, and then one morning I awoke to the realization that I was flat broke. I was forced to sell the plane. The yacht was repossessed. I turned to my wife and her family for assistance, but her answer was a fast move out—to get as far away from me as she could get.

"My clients were enraged. Many lost substantial sums. These same people, many of whom had parlayed small sums into vast fortunes following the advice of Anderson and myself, now cursed my name and harrassed me with threatening phone calls in the night. No one remembered the good old days. As interest rates fluctuated wildly and the stock market plunged in 1974-75, no one mentioned that the record of several other investment experts had also been exceedingly poor during this turbulent era. My world was turned upside down. My friends, my money, my wife—I lost it all.

"The bank finally repossessed the house and furnishings which I had mortgaged in a desperate attempt to hang on until the economy turned around. I was down to my wardrobe. I even sold most of my clothes in order to get enough money to move into a little flea-bag hotel room. People who used to be my friends would look the other way in order to avoid speaking to me on the street.

"Shortly after my wife had divorced me, I telephoned her and asked for a few dollars to keep me going for a week or two. She told me that from the beginning of our relationship she had known I was irresponsible and brainless. She said she married me because she thought I was so wealthy that even an idiot like me could not throw it all into the wind. Her final words cut my soul: 'Don't ever call me or try to contact me again. I despise the mention of your name. Go someplace and hide so the world doesn't have to look at you.'

"I was alone, absolutely alone. I tried to get a job at some of the brokerage houses. They looked at me as if I were crazy. They wanted no part of a loser. The lower I fell, the more bitter I became. How could all these people who had partaken of my wine and bread turn away from me as if I were afflicted with some disease? How could individuals who enjoyed luxuries and lavish parties as the result of my advice now treat me as if I were an idiot?

"I had to get away from everything and everybody associated with my past life. I sought escape through alcohol. I moved downtown, hoping for a new start. I was able to find a job, but after receiving my first paycheck, I went on a drinking binge that lasted a week. My boss gave me another opportunity, but when the same thing happened a few days later, he fired me. I begged, picked up bottles, and shoplifted to get my hands on a few dollars to buy wine. Eventually, I turned to still stronger drugs. The only thing of any importance in my life was escape—escape from reality. Wine, marijuana, cocaine—my total life was the consumption of drugs that would divert my mind from reality and permit me, at least temporarily, to forget my sorry affairs.

"My mind deteriorated rapidly. I lived in constant fear—fear that I would sober up, fear that someone was chasing me, or fear that I was being killed. I remember waking in the night in a cold sweat, believing that I was falling, having jumped off the Golden Gate Bridge. Another time, I thought that I was right in front of a bus which was just about to crush my body. These nightmares were so vivid that I felt they were happening to me at that very moment. This went on night after night. It is a miracle that I didn't kill myself.

"Eventually, broken by the combination of bitterness and drugs, I wound up in the hospital. I was there for almost two weeks and during all that time I did not have one single visitor.

"The only person, besides the doctor and nurses, who seemed to care whether I lived or died was an elderly cleaning lady. One morning she came into the room with a beautiful rose in a vase and placed it on the stand beside my bed. 'I brought you a little flower, Mr. Sebastian,' she said as she reached down to empty the waste basket.

" 'What did you do that for?' I questioned in my usual bellicose manner.

" 'Cause I wanted you to know that I hope you get well and I wanted you to know that someone cares about you,' she replied. She went on, 'God loves each one of us and God loves you, too. I just wanted to make sure that you knew that.'

"After she left the room, I wept. Thoughts crossed my mind. What did she expect to gain? Why was there any reason for her to care about me? It seemed as though the whole world had forsaken me, but here was this sweet lady, for no good reason, taking time to care about me. I felt a warmth that had been absent for years. It occurred to me that I had found a real friend.

"As soon as I left the hospital, I decided to move on to another city. I sold the rest of my clothes in order to get the bus fare that brought me here to this city. I took any odd jobs I could get to buy a little food and pay for my bed at one of the flop houses. However, I was soon to return to my old ways. Again, I turned to alcohol, seeking to dull the hate that I felt for myself and the world around me. I was here for more than a year, I guess, when it happened.

"I had been drinking all day, up until late evening. My body was aching as I lay on the dirty cot. I had been too drunk to make it home the night before and had lain on the cold ground in the park until the early hours of morning. This time I felt that I was at the end of the road. I began to weep, and for the first time in my life I got down on my knees and said over and over again, 'God help me, God help me.' Finally, I was able to go to sleep.

"As I lay there in that dark, dingy hotel room, I began to dream. But this dream was different than ever before. It was as if I were transported to the actual scene of the occurrence.

"As the dream began, I found myself aboard a beautiful luxury yacht. It was a large vessel cutting through the water at full speed. The sky was cloudless and the sea calm. I was on the top deck, and I could hear music coming from below.

"The deck was filled with people sunbathing, drinking, and laughing. It was apparent that I, William Henry Sebastian, was the center of attraction. Every woman that would come near would embrace me. Every man would shake my hand or pat me on the back. Time after time they would raise their glasses to toast me. I was on top of the world.

"I walked below to view a gleaming ballroom filled with dancing couples. Laughter permeated the air. I was pulled onto the dance floor by the most beautiful woman in the room who simply floated across the floor and whispered to

me that I was the greatest man in the world. Soon there was no one on the dance floor but my partner and me. All eyes followed us around the floor as the music played.

"After the dance I again went topside. Clouds were beginning to gather. The wind picked up, and the water rolled and churned. The sky began to blacken. The passengers began to grumble and curse. Still, the storm became worse. The wind and rain was fierce. We all sought refuge below deck as the storm raged and tossed the vessel in the water. Women began to scream, and everyone began to demand that I do something, as if I were responsible for the storm.

"I made my way to the wheel house to find that no one was manning the helm. There was no one in the room. I searched frantically for something that would help me determine where we were heading. There were no maps, no compass, nothing that would give me any direction. I realized I was aboard a ship without a captain or crew, going full speed to nowhere.

"The helm was spinning wildly as the ship plowed through the waves. I took the helm and managed to hold the ship into the wind. Then I heard a scraping, tearing sound. The ship jerked and turned and then suddenly stopped so quickly that I was knocked against the bulkhead of the wheel house. The ship had run aground. The engines were silent.

"I turned to see the crowd of passengers outside the wheelhouse pointing at me and yelling that I had run the ship aground. They grabbed me and carried me to the ship's side. Swinging me by my hands and feet, two men threw me into the ocean. As I entered the water, I looked back toward the ship to see a small beacon of light illuminating the name written on the bow of the ship. It was simply the initials 'W.H.S.'.

"It seemed that I was only in the water a few minutes before my feet touched the bottom and I was able to struggle safely to shore.

"I found myself on a darkened road at dusk. Night was setting in, but there was just enough light to make out the road ahead. Large trees lined the roadside. As I peered down the road into the distance, a bright light was shining. The light was so bright that I couldn't look directly into it. Somehow, it was impressed upon my mind that at the center of this light lay the answer to my problems. If I could reach this light, I would be given the secret-of-secrets.

"My heart was pounding as I began to walk toward the light, but suddenly there loomed up in the path the figure of a man. I couldn't make him out in the darkness, but I could sense the evil as he stood brazenly blocking the path. Behind this creature appeared six dwarfs. Their eyes were shining in the dark. I realized that the man and his helpers would do anything to keep me from travelling down the path toward the light. Each of the dwarfs wore a breastplate. On one was written: 'Fear'. Others were labelled 'Pride', 'Hatred', 'Slothfulness', 'Envy', and 'Greed'. There was a breastplate on the larger creature, too, but I could not see well enough to make it out. I stood there trembling, wishing to move toward the light, but fearful of the dreadful creatures blocking the way.

"As I waited, I was taken from the path to the castle of the richest man in the world. The castle was surrounded with a fortress wall. Guards patrolled the wall, and huge dogs were in front of the wall, threatening to tear to shreds anyone who might come near the castle. Inside, the richest man in the wojld was sitting in the middle of a mountain of money. He was counting his treasures. I could hear him say over and over, 'This is mine. This is mine. This is mine.'

"The scene suddenly shifted, and I was given another view of the life of the rich man. This time the scene was his funeral. Death had taken him, just as it had billions of others—both rich and poor—before him. As I viewed the corpse, I asked, 'How much did he leave?'

" 'All of it.' The answer came back from those at the funeral.

"After the funeral I was taken to the burial ground of this, the richest man in the world. While his grave was headed with huge marble stone, there was no name on the stone. He, like many others, was a non-entity. Once he was gone people had forgotten who he was. However, there was writing on the stone:

'For what is a man profited, if he shall gain the whole world, and lose his own soul?' (Matthew 16:26)

"The scene shifted back to the narrow path with

the bright light in the distance. The large creature was snarling and making ready for battle. The creatures behind him were snapping and clawing at the ground in their eagerness to devour me. Somehow, I had gained a renewed will to survive and was determined to go forward to the light. As I moved toward the larger creature, I was suddenly aware of the dreadful name written across the breast: 'Self'. As I looked in the face of the creature, what I saw was a shock, almost too heavy to bear. It was my face!

" 'My God, how could it be,' I wondered. The abhorrent creature that I had so easily recognized in others was also within me. I resisted. 'Not me, not me!' I shouted. I have always been generous. I was always the first to pick up the tab! The drinks and food were always on me. The yacht, the plane and my home were always open to our customers and friends.

"A voice came back from the distant light, 'Foolish man, with eyes that cannot see, you are totally selfish. When have you reached down to lift up a fellow stranger? When have you searched out and comforted the lonely, the old or the sick? Tell me when you have reached out your hand to touch the needy or placed bread at the table of the hungry? When did you offer your coat to a man without a coat?"

"I awoke. As I sat there I became vividly aware, for the first time in my life, that I had never freely given anything that didn't hold the promise of reward or praise. I saw the real William Henry Sebastian, face to face. It was an ugly face. By this time I was half awake and half asleep. It was as if the dream were reality. I put my face into the pillow and wept in repentence. As I asked God to forgive me for the selfishness that had dominated my entire life, I felt a new focus come into my life. I began to realize that success could only be achieved through giving with no hope of reward.

"I really did not fully understand this truth, but I believed it.

"As I lay in bed contemplating this great truth, I drifted off to sleep again. I was brought back to the darkened path. Now, I was more determined than ever to advance down the path toward the light. My courage strengthened. I moved toward the ugly creature and the six dwarfs, filled with the faith that I was going to find the light. As I proceeded fearlessly toward the creatures, my hand grasped at the one called 'Selfishness'. But I grasped only thin air. The creature vanished. The dwarfs, too, had disappeared.

"Warmth came over me. I was standing in the light. The light had come to me. I looked ahead to the source of the light, and at that point, the 'Secret for the Ages' was suddenly before my eyes. For a swift moment, I was able to view the very heart of the light, so brilliant with radiance and power that only a glance was possible.

"I awoke again.

"To this day, I can recall vividly the astounding revelation that was branded into my consciousness, affecting my whole being. I was humbled to realize that I had been chosen to view this marvelous truth—a truth so simple that the entire world already possesses the knowledge. Many have been taught the concept from birth even though they have never accepted and acknowledged the truth in their lives.

"I realized for the first time in my life that God and love are the same thing. The light was so radiant, yet it emanated from the shadow of the cross! Immediately I understood pure love. Without being motivated by self-interest or gain, God sent his Son to die on the cross for our sins.

"This was love beyond human comprehension. This was the greatest love story of all time. And it is God's plan that we would be as much like Him as possible. He expects us to love—to help bring happiness into the lives of others, even as He had done so. Suddenly, I knew that nothing in life mattered more than love—love of God and love for one's fellow man.

"I realized why my life had been such a failure. I realized that real happiness is possible only when we live our lives in harmony with God. God has certain laws that are universally true. If we do not conduct our lives within the framework of God's laws, tragedy, disappointment and unhappiness will result. If one's life is not in harmony with God's laws for successful living, failure is the inevitable outcome. To be out of harmony with God is to be decaying and dying. To harmonize with God is to live eternally.

"I just sat there on the bed, staring into the

emptiness, my mind captured by the dream that had just unfolded. The scene replayed in my mind on a giant movie screen. Each time the light would flash I could see the shadow of the cross issuing from its source. I knew what the cross meant.

"I remembered listening to a country preacher in a little mountain church, sitting beside my beloved Leilani. I don't recall ever having considered his message seriously since that time, but I could hear his call vividly: 'No matter what your trouble may be, no matter how low you may have gone, ask Jesus to come into your heart and He will take your burdens away and give you a peace that passeth understanding.'

"I just closed my eyes and prayed, 'Jesus, I come to you without knowing much about you, but I believe that you are the Son of God and that you died for me, for my sins. I ask you now to come into my heart.'

"The lamp was still burning in my room. I looked around at the mess and was aware of the stench in the place, most of it coming from me. I had been living in darkness and was not aware of the creeping evil that had engulfed my life. Since I had stood in the light, I was now able to see my condition, and it was abhorrent. I could not wait to do something about it. It was urgent! I had gone through an inward cleansing and found I could not tolerate the outward filth. Before morning, I had picked up, cleaned up and scrubbed up everything from the wall to the floors. After the room was cleaned, I had the longest and greatest shower I have ever enjoyed.

"The next morning I found the cleanest clothes I could find and dressed for the day. When I stepped out, I heard birds singing. I felt a warm breeze on my face. I touched a flower and wondered at the miracle. When had I last noticed these simple wonders? I was a new creature seeing with new eyes. I was enjoying a peace that passes all understanding.

"I said 'Good Morning' to those I passed on the street, and you know, they were smiling and returning my greetings. My heart was pounding with joy at the prospect of somehow expressing love. I felt a compulsion to give of myself. The question was—What could I give?

"That question remained in my mind for only a

moment. The offices of the local blood bank came into view. I knew instantly where my giving would begin. I walked into the blood bank and offered blood. The aide promised, as I instructed, to donate the pint of blood to the first poor person who needed it.

"Since I had been privileged to view the secret of the ages, I found a Christian book store and purchased a Bible. The sales lady was such a warm, lovely person. The way this lady treated me made me feel completely whole again. She was the first woman with whom I had carried on a lengthy conversation since I started my fast slide to the gutter.

"I opened up my heart to her. I told of my wretched life and about my dream of the past evening. Tears of joy filled her eyes as I told her of my compulsion to reach out and help other people.

"That evening as I returned to the old rooming house in which I was staying, several of the derelicts rooming there were in the sitting room. All had been drinking, and the smell of vomit filled my nostrils. They offered me a drink which I refused. They looked at me as if they were seeing a stranger. It was apparent that the change I felt inside was showing outwardly.

"One of the men asked where I had been. I responded by saying that I had been on a marvelous, exciting journey. I told them that I had discovered the 'Secret of the Ages.' You wouldn't believe the attention I received as I told them about the dream. Every man followed me to the room to see how I had cleaned it up.

"That evening, as I retired to bed, I set some goals that I determined I would carry out during the next few months. The first was that I would find temporary employment and that I would keep only ten percent for my needs and would use the other ninety percent to reach out and help the needy. I would also work to help change the lives of all eight derelicts who stayed at the rooming house. I believed I already knew the basic problem—each man there believed that no one cared whether they lived or died. Nobody cared! Their enemy was loneliness. They were lonely because they were unable to recognize the depravity that completely dominated their lives.

"Finally, I would return to the brokerage business within the next two months. I had lost it all in the brokerage business because of selfishness and unsound business practices. The new Sebastian would now practice the opposite principles.

"I awoke early the next morning, shaved, bathed, and dressed for the day. I opened the door to leave the room and was surprised to see Jimmy, a young man in his twenties, in the doorway just down the hall. He beckoned me to his room. He had shaved and bathed. I was thrilled as I looked around. His room was as clean as could be. Grinning broadly, Jimmy informed me that he had cleaned all night. 'It's strange but the filth didn't bother me until last night. Thanks, Sebastian', he said.

"I left the building a jubilant man. I had affected another life for the better.

"At a nearby grocery store, I cajoled the manager into letting me sweep floors in exchange for a sack of food. I took this food and added the last few dollars in my possession to purchase another sack of food. With the food sacks in hand I walked around by the railroad tracks through row after row of skid row homes until I came to an old shack, unpainted, with several boards missing on the side. A old man and woman were sitting on the porch. Without introducing myself, I told them that I had felt led to bring food to them. The tears that came from those precious old people would have gladdened the heart of anyone.

"I took a job washing dishes in a restaurant. For two months my main purpose in life was focused on one thing—giving. I would take the money I earned, buy food and carry it to some needy family. I never revealed who I was or where I came from. I had found this passage in the Bible I had purchased and which I now read regular-ly:

'Take heed that ye do not your alms before men, to be seen of them: Otherwise ye have no reward of your Father which is in Heaven. Therefore when thou doest thine alms, do not sound a trumpet before thee, as the hypocrites do in the synagogues and in the streets, that they may have glory of men. Verily I say unto you, they have their reward. But when thou doest alms, let not thy left hand know what thy right hand

doeth: That thine alms may be in secret: And thy Father which seeth in secret himself will reward you openly.' (Matthew 6:1-4)

"Each evening I would return to the rooming house. I would bring food for the men when I could afford it. We would sit around and talk of past experiences, and I would read a little Scripture before we retired.

"The lady from the bookstore, Miss Sara Vaughn, was becoming a close friend. Many evenings she would come over and join in the conversation. The presence of this godly lady was an inspiration. I never saw anyone take a drink or act disrespectful during her visits.

"One by one, I could see a change in all the lives in that boarding house. Within six weeks the house itself was changed from a flea-bag dwelling to a decent place to live. We had cleaned up the sitting room. The owner was kind enough to give us paint, so we painted the house inside and out. One by one, each of my friends at the boarding house changed to the point of returning to a productive life.

"During the three months following my dream,

I devoted my time completely to helping the needy. I was happier and more content with life than during the peak of my financial success.

"After three months, as I had planned, I returned to my home town. I wanted to go back and see my old friends and customers and to reveal to them the change that had taken place in me. To many, I wanted to ask forgiveness. I went first to my old office. After introducing myself to the receptionist, I asked if I could see John Anderson. To my surprise, John burst out of his office, put his arms around me and invited me to come in and sit down. I spent more than two hours telling John about my miserable drunken life and relayed to him the experience that had changed my life. This good man was as excited as I had ever seen him. He called his secretary and asked her to dust off my old desk. He reached into the desk drawer and placed on the desk the plate with the name "William Henry Sebastian'

" 'Bill', he started, 'I am taking it for granted that you are ready to go back to work. I have thought about it since you left, and I have concluded that if you had not trusted me as your broker at the beginning of our relationship, I would never have achieved the financial success I enjoy today.' He sat there, wrote out a check for ten thousand dollars, and handed it to me. 'You can consider this a loan; however, should misfortune strike you again, I will never approach you for payment. I feel I owe you this.'

"I went to work that day. I called old friends and customers. I relayed my new-found experience to each of them. With John Anderson's welcomed advice, my business began to prosper. I am travelling a great deal now. You might say that our business has taken an international flavor. I also give lectures on my experience. I pray that my only motive in telling this story will remain—to touch the lives of all who will listen, that they also might experience the satisfaction of living a less selfish life.

"I am deeply moved to know that many who have heard my story have experienced dramatic changes in their own lives as they adopted the principles of giving. People on the verge of a nervous breakdown have become whole again simply by filling the void in their lives by developing concern for others. Problems vanish as they reach out to touch an orphan or attend some aged soul. Families once torn by jealousy and hate have found a renewed love and enjoyment of life as they took an interest in a local children's home or a needy stranger."

Sebastian paused again, as if considering whether or not to go on. He began again.

"Even though I was experiencing a satisfaction that I had never known, the memory of Leilani Webster would not fade from my consciousness. After more than twenty years I would spend hours at night reliving my short time with Leilani in those Tennessee hills and dreaming of things that might have been.

"Six months after my return to Chicago, I flew to Nashville for a business trip. Something compelled me to rent a car and drive back toward the place where I had met and courted Leilani. I wanted to see the old Webster home and walk, once again, to the cliff that over-looked the waterfall where I had known perfect love and, yes, the place where Leilani had plunged to her death.

"Uneasily, but eagerly, I turned off on the road that led to the Webster home. The area had changed. There were more houses and more of the land had been cleared for farming. I was about a mile from the Webster home when a small shopping center came into view. The center had a grocery store, a hardware store, a drug store and a beauty salon.

"I drove the car into the center and walked into the hardware store. A young man behind the cash register was the only one in the store. I asked him if he knew Daniel and Sara Webster. He said he hadn't lived in the area long and didn't know many people. He didn't know Dan and Sara. He said, however, that a lady named Webster owned the beauty shop at the other end of the center. He didn't know her first name.

"I walked over to the beauty shop and went in. There were a couple of ladies under the hair dryers, and the beautician was behind a divider shampooing someone. I could only see her head and the upper part of her face. She looked up as I closed the door behind me. She only gave me a glance as she returned to her work.

" 'Can I help you?' she asked.

"The voice from behind the screen startled me.

It sounded like the voice—no, it couldn't be— the voice of Leilani Webster.

" 'Sir, can I help you?' she asked the second time.

"I could barely speak. 'Do you know Daniel and Sara Webster?' I asked haltingly.

" 'Yes,' she answered. 'I am their daughter, Leilani.'

"She had not finished speaking before I hurried past the divider. Trembling, I asked, 'You're Leilani?'

"She turned and I almost fainted. Leilani Webster was looking at me with those unforgetable green eyes, wide and disbelieving.

" 'William?'

"Tears were rolling down my cheeks. 'Yes', I nodded, 'I am William Sebastian.'

"We embraced, faces wet with tears. We stood and looked at each other, oblivious to those around us.

" 'Leilani, I can't believe that I have just touched you. For more than twenty years I have believed you were dead.'

"The customer at the shampoo bowl was getting impatient. Leilani asked me to wait until she hurriedly finished with the customer.

"I watched her as she combed and styled the woman's hair. The way she had retained her youthful appearance was remarkable. I knew she must be about thirty-eight years old, yet I could see no lines in her face. As she moved about the shop, continually smiling and glancing in my direction, I could see that her still trim body and graceful movements were as I remembered.

"I sat there in a daze. Even though, at this point, I did not know whether Leilani was married or would consider having me play any part in her life, I felt as if the most important dream of my life was somehow coming true. How I had asked myself time and again—if only I could have been given another chance. I was completely confused, but soon I would learn the cruel hoax that fate had played on both of us.

"After the customer left, I told her how I fought coming back to her, and how after a year I met old Isaac on the road, and how he had told me she had committed suicide by jumping from the cliff overlooking the waterfall.

" 'Poor Isaac,' she recalled. 'About six months after you left the mountains, he just went crazy. The man had all kinds of hallucinations. Before he died about three years later, he began to believe he was Daniel Boone. Sometimes he would not recognize me and had told several people that I had committed suicide.'

"Leilani said that it was true that for many months she had walked to the cliff daily to reminisce. It was also true that she was so depressed and disappointed about my not returning that she couldn't eat for a short time. She said, however, that time began to remove some of the hurt, but she had never loved another man. As old Isaac had stated, 'I had stole her heart'.

"I told Leilani about the wretched life that almost destroyed me and about the dream that had changed me.

"Later that evening we drove down to see her

parents who were old but still active and alert. We spent a wonderful evening together. I rented a room in a motel a few miles from the Webster home. For two weeks I renewed my relationship with Leilani. I felt twenty years younger. I felt completely fulfilled.

"I asked Leilani to marry me and she accepted again. We were married at her parents' home and flew back to Chicago the same day. She is now my constant companion, my paradise completed."

Sebastian stopped briefly to nod to a group of teenagers strolling loudly through the park. He was almost finished.

"I feel that to tell you about my own personal giving would violate God's law of silence on this subject. I would like to say, however, that as I have reached out with my heart to help others, the resources to do so have returned to me in a flood. Through my desire for God to reduce the greed in my heart, he has given me an understanding about business that has caused me to prosper beyond my fondest dreams. As the Scripture teaches,

'Give, and it shall be given unto you; good measure, pressed down, and shaken together, and running over, shall men give into your bosom. For with the same measure that ye mete withal it shall be measured to you again.' (Luke 6:38)

"All in all, I am at peace. I pray I will never be so busy that I cannot take the time to search out those who are less fortunate than I and help them."

As Mr. Sebastian was speaking, his black limousine entered the park. It drove to our area and stopped. The chauffeur stepped out and stood by the left front.

Sebastian bade my farewell, walked to the limousine, and conversed with the driver for a moment. They entered the vehicle and drove toward the entrance.

As I watched the car disappear, I wondered if I would ever see him again. I knew I had been in the presence of an unusual man. In only a few minutes he had convinced me that the opposite of what the world believes is true. Success, peace and happiness do not depend on what you get but what you give.

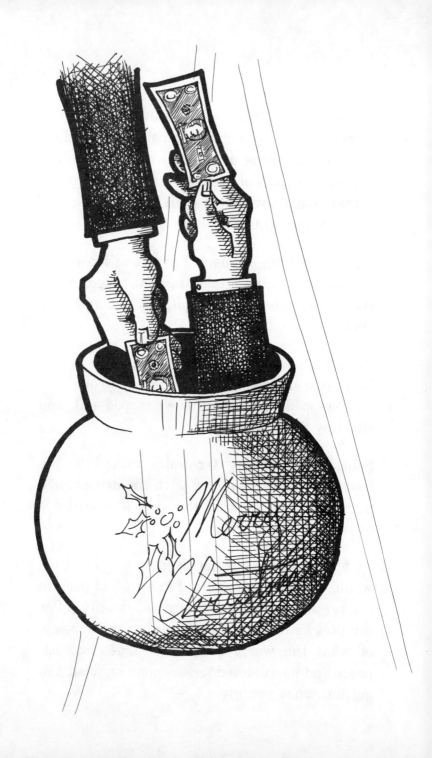

After Sebastian drove away, I sat in that small community park and pondered the story I had just heard. It was a beautiful warm day. The sun was shining. A light breeze ruffled the leaves. The birds were singing. The whisper of water flowing over the rocks and the laughter of children playing in the grass brought a tranquil spirit to the park.

The sound of a yapping dog drew my attention to a cluster of garbage cans about fifty yards down the walk to my right. A bum was rummaging through the cans in search of food. I did something that would have been completely out of character for me only a few minutes before. I walked over and patted him on the shoulder. As I looked into his sad, hopeless eyes I knew that I had a wonderful opportunity.

"Sir, would you grant me the favor of buying your lunch today?"

EPILOGUE

Not long ago I drove down to Pelham, South Carolina. This had been my world as a child. I can't recall travelling more than 20 miles from Pelham before I was fourteen.

A friend was with me on this trip. We drove across the Reedy River bridge past rows of unpainted houses and the ruins of the old burned out cotton mill. My friend was amused by my excitement and chuckled as he pointed to an outhouse. "What compels you to return to this place?" he asked.

I pondered this for a moment. "Memories," I answered simply.

My mom and dad, a brother, and six sisters lived in a four room cottage. As we approached the old homestead, I could visualize my mom stirring clothes in an old iron pot. It took a whole day to do a week's wash for a family of ten. Each time I return I am trying to go back

home, back where love was born. I am paying
homage to a memory.

It is in fact from these memories that William
Henry Sebastian emerges. The story of Sebastian embodies the central truths which have
framed my life. Unlike Sebastian, I started
without much. But I learned the same lessons.

Our family had little, but we seldom com-
plained. Dad worked on the W.P.A. during the
depression. After times got better he got on at
the cotton mill. He found Christ when I was
nine, and a year later he was preaching. There
wasn't much money in any of this.

But we all helped. In the summer the children
would search the fields and woods for wild
berries. My brother and I shot or trapped wild
rabbit and squirrel. Our shirts and dresses were
made of flour sacks, but we were not ashamed.
Most of the folks in the community were
wearing the same thing. The flour companies
even made the bags in different patterns so we
wouldn't all be wearing the same color.

This was before television, of course. My
pastimes were playing cowboys and Indians and
going to the creek. The most exciting thing I
remember was when the old cotton mill burned
down. To me it seemed as if the whole world was
on fire. Another time it was rumored that a

small plane was going to land in Ward's
pasture. The whole community turned out.
After viewing the bumpy field, the pilot chick-
ened out. It was a big disappointment.

These childhood memories focus on events
that the adults involved might think would be
forgotten in a day, but they are often burned
into the memory of a child, like the time Elsie
Davis saw the hunger or delight in my four-
year-old eyes and gave me a chocolate bunny
from the showcase.

One experience, which helped frame my
understanding of giving, parallels Sebastian's
gift to the child in the park. I was about nine.
Our school was having a candy sale, and I
wanted to do my part. I brought a box home, but
Dad was afraid I would lose the bars or have
them stolen, and he couldn't afford to pay for
them. I told him I would be especially careful.

I walked to the village to try to sell some
candy. Several big boys were playing in the
yard at the first house. "Want to buy some
candy?" I asked.

One of the boys took the box and passed it
around. It came back empty. They just laughed.

I didn't know what to do. I knew I would be
punished. As I walked home, frightened and
crying, a man standing in his yard asked what

was wrong. I explained what happened and showed him the empty box.

"Stop crying, Son," he said. "I'll pay for the candy." He gave me forty-five cents, a lot of money in those days. You could buy a week's groceries for three dollars. He gave without any hope or desire of reward, except to see a frightened boy smile.

I never saw him again, but later in life I tracked him down to thank him and called him in another city. His name is Carrol Fleming. This retired preacher didn't remember me or the candy, but it occured to me that this event, so important in the eyes of a child, was possibly an everyday practice for Mr. Fleming.

My next major lesson in giving occurred years later at a time of desperation. After leaving school in the ninth grade to work in the mill, I had joined the Navy at seventeen. Then I had come back to the mill for a few months but was able to get on the police force in Greenville. But marriage and a first child made times hard. I took some odd jobs but couldn't escape the dream of a nice home and car, even if it was financed.

I decided to go into sales. The first months were terrible. I knew my product and thought I was giving a terrific sales pitch, but nothing happened. When another vehicle hit the back of my old Oldsmobile, I had to use the settlement money to pay bills and buy groceries. Driving around in the wrecked car confirmed my feelings of frustration. It's human nature to resist buying from a failure.

I was devastated and had reapplied for my old police job, when an acquaintance invited me to hear Dr. Napoleon Hill. I had never heard of this great author and philosopher, so I declined. "Gun Smoke" was on TV that night. But after persistant urging, I agreed to go. Only about 15 people showed up.

Hill was not an imposing figure. He was a short, gray-haired old gentleman without a strong, commanding voice. But he spoke with a power derived from knowledge. He said men become what they think. He said that whatever you planted in your mind would grow there. He insisted that whatever the mind of a man could conceive and believe, he could achieve.

These thoughts alone began to alter my understanding, but he addressed more specifically the reason for my failure in sales. He pointed out that the only way you could extend your business was to extend your service. His advice was to forget about the money you could extract from your customer and concentrate on helping and serving him. He talked about other concepts as well, like visualizing one's dreams, but it was this concept that intrigued me most. What I had been doing was like standing before a stove saying, "Stove, give me heat," without putting in the wood and fire.

I couldn't wait until my first call the next day. It was a large beauty salon. The owner was nice enough, but she would usually say, "Good morning, Mr. Good. Thanks for stopping by, but we don't need anything. If we do, we'll call."

As I drove to the shop, I was thinking about the shop owner and what I could do to help her. I thought about volunteering to clean a hair dryer. As I walked in the door, there were no thoughts of rejection in my mind. The first thing she did was invite me back to the lounge area for a cup of coffee. The only thing I was doing differently was thinking differently. Within two weeks my world was turning around. This was my first indication that success is determined by what you give and not what you get.

During this period I began to realize that what Dr. Hill had taught and what other writers in different "success" books I was reading were saying was, whether they were aware of it or not, promoting a philosophy based on the Bible.

The Scriptures weave the fabric of God's infallible law, the law of compensation—the success factor. Luke 6:38 states this law precisely:

Give and it shall be given unto you; good measure, pressed down and running over, shall men give to your bosom. For with the same measure that ye mete withall, it shall be measured to you again.

This verse is the key to a better life, not only in the next life, but in this one. Doesn't it seem strange that many who will tell you they believe the Bible from cover to cover spend their lives carrying an empty sack while they are also carrying the secret around in their hands, the Holy Bible?

It isn't really all that strange, however. There is a basic selfishness in man which prevents him from seeing the truth. A man may sincerely read the Scriptures and not even see what it says because it contradicts Greed's mistaken view of success. Greed says "take" to get gain. The Bible says "give." The world programs us for failure.

Something happened to me recently that illustrates how easily we can be programmed. I drove to Gulf Breeze, Florida, for a routine contact and drove down 14th Ave. I turned left on Gregory St. like I had many times before, and an officer pulled me over within a few hundred yards and informed me that I was going the wrong way on a one-way street. I told him that if the street had been changed, it should have been more clearly marked. Chuckling, he asked me to drive back to the intersection and look at the markers. I was amazed to see a sign almost as large as a billboard clearly identifying the one-way street. Likewise, many people can not see the road to success which has been so clearly marked.

My own faith was not as sudden as Sebastian's. Giving to the church and to my fellow man began with some pain. Even though I had some knowledge of the secret with respect to my business, it took a little experience to know that God's law of compensation worked in every area of life. When I dropped a bill in the offering plate I felt that worth was being extracted from me, when all the time God was reaching in and taking greed out.

But I have learned that the law of giving always works. To give and not receive is impossible. We should be able to give without thought of reward, but as we practice the law we begin to know that reward is coming. The seed of reward is already within the deed.

Our understanding of these concepts is often clouded, particularly with respect to money. We think that because "the love of money is the root of all evil" and because it is "easier for a camel to go through the eye of a needle than for a rich man to enter into the kingdom of God," then money itself is evil. The camel-needle-rich-man passage is recorded in Matthew 19:16-30. A careful reading of this passage indicates that a rich, young ruler wanted to inherit eternal life. The condition Christ laid down was that he must sell all that he had and give it to the poor. Jesus knew that his heart was centered in his possessions. The message was that no man could reach the kingdom of God who trusted in riches.

Actually, the law of compensation was the issue. The rich man, in his greed, believed that to follow Christ would clean him out when, in fact, his possessions would only be absent as long as it took to extract the greed from his heart. He left "very sorrowful, for he was very rich;" but if he had stayed around to hear the end of the sermon, he would have heard Christ teach that whatever we give up we shall receive "manifold more in this present time, and in the world to come, life everlasting."

There are few people in our society that are not more comfortable, and indeed richer, than this rich, young ruler. He could not afford a car or an air conditioner. The problem was not the wealth or the degree of wealth; the problem was the heart.

It should be emphasized that God's law of compensation does not diminish other rules which govern success such as the importance of maintaining a positive attitude, or having enthusiasm, imagination, initiative, self-control, self-confidence, concentration, tolerance and vision. Actually these traits emerge as love and service become focal points in our lives.

This does not even require money. Sebastian began by donating blood and time, commodities we all possess. The real gift is love. When we begin to concentrate on developing this virtue, we find that, like the creatures in Sebastian's dream, our problems begin to vanish. I have known people who, because of greed, turned inward and suffered from great fear, but when forced to care for a loved one came out of deep depression within days.

This happens because love produces compassion, charisma, efficiency, grace, serenity, fairness, responsibility, loyalty, courage, honesty, cleanliness, moderation, industry, resolution and many other virtues. On the other hand, greed produces indigestion, fatigue, frigidity, headaches, and ulcers physically, coupled with fear, intolerance, egotism, jealousy, impatience, anger, lust, indecision, dishonesty, and cruelty. Yet we are so programed to act as society expects us to act that we find it difficult to change. When we are kicked, we want to kick back. Greed and conformity act as barriers which prevent us from expressing love to others. We can not seem to sing the song of the universe, love. We hold back, waiting to see if we will be loved in return, still desiring to get instead of to give.

This is seen in the love parents often extend to their children. We desire that they behave in a certain way and demand this behavior as a proof of their love and a condition for ours. It is difficult at first to escape from this kind of conditional love, but if we begin to practice the principles of giving anyway, we notice a change in ourselves and eventually a change in the attitude of others toward us. Once we begin to "do unto others" as we would have them do unto us, we are opening the door to success.

I wish I could say that this is the way I

approach all my relationships with others, but of course it isn't, although I like to think I am becoming consistently better. One event several years ago, however, has become my personal standard and example.

I had called on a large beauty shop every other week for many years. The owner had been a good friend, but one week there were some questions about a shipment. She asked if I thought she was lying about the problem.

"No, I don't think you're lying."

"Yes, you do," she insisted.

I didn't know what to say or do so I left, hoping that by the time I made the next call she would cool down. But the next time I came by, she wrote out the check without even looking up from her desk. She didn't say a word.

"Aren't you going to say 'good morning'?" I asked.

She looked up with an anger I had never seen before. "I hate your guts!" was all she said.

I was stunned. I stood there for at least 30 seconds before I spoke. My silent reaction was to lash out, but I didn't.

"I don't hate you. I love you," I said. "I couldn't hate you after all these years you have given me your business and your friendship. If you will tell me what I've done to hurt you, I'll get down on my knees right here in front of your customers and ask your forgiveness."

She didn't say anything. I told her I didn't want to bug my friends so we could square up our accounts on my next visit, and I wouldn't bother her anymore.

The next time I called she met me with a love and warmth that has cemented a wonderful friendship for many years. Had I loved her with conditions or, worse yet, reacted in kind, we might be enemies today.

This is, in the end, the success factor—learning to give—learning to love. It is our fantasy, our heart's desire, to be loved. Others want—and need—the same thing. We should learn to concentrate on the giving. Be assured that the response will be love returned, multiplied many fold. The next lonely soul you should meet, who, like Sebastian, seems to be filled with anger and hate, needs to see evidence that someone cares. A seed of kindness should be sown. If you are to be that someone, then you will most surely reap a good harvest.